As a Sailboat Seeks the Wind

COLLECTED WRITINGS

MARIAN A. KELNER

BOOKSMYTH PRESS
Shelburne Falls, MA

Published in the United States by Booksmyth Press of
Shelburne Falls, MA 01370 [www.thebooksmyth.com]
Author may be contacted at marian.kelner@gmail.com

ISBN 978-0-9815830-3-7

Book and cover design by Maureen Moore
Illustrations by Julie Ariel Schochet
Cover art: Portion of *Sailing* by Thomas Eakins from a photographic
reproduction in Wickimedia, no known copyright restrictions.

This book is dedicated to

all the miraculous beings sharing this Earth with us humans
and
my sisters, friends, and animal family who have been
with me through brisk winds, sweet summer breezes,
doldrums, and hurricanes.

You shall continue to seek experiences
as a sailboat seeks the wind

~ *a dream message*

Contents

One: Animals and Nature

Two: Fact and Fiction

Three: Family

Four: Inner World

Five: Politics

ONE

ANIMALS and NATURE

I Swam into Autumn

I swam into autumn
in the river of swallows
in the river of geese.

On a late August morning
I swam into autumn
gliding up river
into the first yellow leaves
drifting downstream.

Sunday Morning Communion

Weeds grow in cracks
where asphalt and concrete meet;
a sparse gray pipe forest stands
where parking meters once stood.

This lot, half-empty,
is so peaceful, birds standing
on the concrete divide
stretch up to eat dangling seeds
from wild grass –
their soft bellies
open to the world.

This autumn sun is perfectly warm.
This ice tea perfectly cold.
This chocolate melting in my mouth
the perfect wafer for
this Sunday morning communion.

Illusion

That we are all one
seems so clear,
seeing the grasses,
the trees,
flowing from their birthing places
along this one ground.

But for us,
who bubble up
to glide,
to float,
to move tethered
one foot at a time,
oneness eludes us.

But today, walking the land,
I receive this message:
We have not been exiled.
We have been tossed up
in gestures of joy and celebration
by the one
who has never really
let us go.

Love in Beauty

Seeking love in beauty,
I've fallen to my knees
to hear the endless seas
rush messages ashore.
They wash away the small
and break against these walls.

I sense where love resides,
that tenderness prevails,
when witnessing high tides
and feeling lost and small,
I lift and set my sails
and float across these walls.

I feel the silent waves
beneath the sizzling foam
hold creatures great and small,
and come to know breath saves
as breezes take me home
on flowing liquid walls.

Great love I see resides
in beauty vast and small.
I find it in the world.
I touch it with my hands
above the shifting sands,
beneath the shifting walls.

Squirrels

I COULD TELL THIS SQUIRREL WAS MALE as he relieved himself on my kitchen storm window, having first leapt from the ground to the side of the house and then to the top screen. Now he has grabbed the bird feeder and settled upside down to leisurely eat one sunflower seed after another.

As I assessed the damage, it was evident he had done this before. I had wondered why it was becoming increasingly difficult to see through the window and why there were vertical lines on the wood siding. And here was the answer, hanging by his hind legs staring me straight in the eye as he cracked open his fifteenth seed.

This squirrel was not a lone marauder. He had a good friend and an acquaintance and, it turned out, these three gave the birds access to the food supply only when they dropped like heavy fruit to the ground and toddled off to sleep.

I don't know why I didn't move the feeder. I did receive intermittent rewards seeing birds perched in the nearby bushes waiting and waiting, and then making adventurous forays to the ground or darting to the feeder to find a leftover seed or two.

I do have a soft spot for squirrels, I admit. I empathize with their daily brushes with death as they cross the roads running between their bedrooms and kitchens. I want to make life easier for them. So I bought bag after bag of sunflower seeds. Threw old bread out my back door. Watched the shells mount in archeological strata.

I realized I had created a monster one warm day when I returned home to find a squirrel in my dining room. Although I encouraged him to run out the open door, he opted for a screened window, ripped a hole in it, and popped out. I noted a matching entry hole in the screen on the opposite wall.

The word, it seems, was out on the squirrel grapevine. This structure, my house, was a giant bird feeder, a huge cereal box. Squirrels were now trying to get in the front, back, and sides of the house. They punched holes in the ground floor screens and, in spectacular acrobatic leaps, soared to the second floor from nearby bushes, dug their claws in, and slid down leaving machete-like rips behind.

Okay, I said. Enough is enough. No more food. No more bird feeder. No more open windows until they get the message this is my territory, not theirs.

The squirrels continued coming around for a while, climbing through the screens before bumping their heads against the unexpected glass. But eventually their interest waned and they kept a low profile, except for that day when the male was chasing the female trying to mate - twenty minutes of chatter while racing up one branch, down onto another, out on a limb, with the female then leaping over the male and then back up, down, and out again until finally they mated in less than 10 seconds on my neighbor's tree trunk.

My heart softened. I need to nourish the pregnant female, I think. But now it is by throwing an apple core or two down the hill, sometimes under the cover of night, so they don't associate the food with my house.

I am, however, aware of the squirrels watching me. Last week I heard one bump her head against the living room window, and when I throw the apple cores, they are there within a minute. But these are attempts of last resort until the weather gets rough, when, if I know myself at all, I'll head out to the pines and throw some seeds their way.

The Spider and the Sacrament

As the sun is rising,
I step across the narrow space you inhabit
between the ramp and
where the boats are tied each night.

I have seen you now and then,
huge, dark,
scary, most people would say,
but to me, majestic, mysterious,
with your eight legs,
bristling body,
absolute silence.

Stretched across your territory,
I see you climb out of the darkness
and settle on the warming wood
by my hand.

And so we lie
side by side,
having emerged from different nights,
about to live different days.

Arms, legs radiating from our bodies,
we receive the blessings of the first light.

The Cardinal

The feet,
once curled around slender branches,
stretch toward an endless sky.

The wings,
moments ago flashes of red in soft sunlit woods,
are splayed against the black asphalt,
this bird splashed dead in the middle of the road.

The cardinal's mate flies alone,
gliding into a small tree by the roadside
in the early morning light.

Had she spent the night,
head tilted to one side,
listening for the beat of familiar wings,
for a call in the night air?

Had she slept,
waking suddenly to the jab of space by her side?

Had she searched beneath the stars,
in the vastness of stunning absence,
in the hollows of sudden disappearance?

Sonnet for Anya

Running as fast as your life force can go,
You leap without weight and dance through the pines,
Footprints embedded in untrodden snow,
The remnants of choices in scattered lines.
If happiness searched for a home on earth,
Eyeing clear dewdrops and wildflower plains,
It would find in you a place for rebirth,
A refuge from the source of turmoil's pain.
It would meet its own kind in your deep joy
At being alive on a winter's day
With the smells of mice as intriguing toys
Beneath small hills of autumn's browned bent hay.
   Golden dog abounding in ecstasy
    Jumping skyward with love leaping from thee.

My Next Life

I N MY NEXT LIFE I WILL BE THE BARK of a tree growing in a hemlock forest. I will feel the sway of the wind, the heat of the sun, the ping of the first snowfall, the hammering of a flicker, the tickle of insect feet, the clasp of squirrels circling and leaping.

In my next life I will be part of the earth, soaking in the rain, drying out, covered with leaves. I will feel the animals that walk upon me and the animals that live within me. I will feel the roots of trees as they burrow and the stretching of the grasses as they emerge into the springtime air.

In my next life I will be part of a wild bird who flies through the trees, soars through the nighttime sky, spirals in the wind, builds a home in the crook of a tree and wakes up in an ocean of leaves in the early morning light.

In my next life I will be a drop in the ocean filtered through the gills of fish, sucked into the mouth of a whale, drawn into clouds in ecstatic evaporation, tumbled in a creek, ingested by a rhinoceros and peed out onto the savannahs of Africa.

In my next life I will be a molecule of air circling the planet, pulled into the bodies of those who breathe me in. I will travel on rivers of blood, used in brain cells to create thought, in muscles to create movement, and then, released, I will swirl through climates until I am drawn into the nose of a mouse and then a panda bear and then a businessman hurrying down the streets of Tokyo.

The Rabbit and the Lion

I cannot leave her in her cage.
I let the rabbit go.
There she runs white and eager
into the thickness of the forest.

The green glow of the pines
envelop her and soon she is gone
and it is silent.

I fear the worst:
that in her first moments of freedom,
heart beating fast,
scared and exhilarated,
she has zigzagged
into the hungry mouth of death.

Then from among the trees,
walking toward me,
comes a female lion,
slow, powerful, purposeful.
I can do nothing
but relax and let my acceptance
meet her power.

She moves close, nose to nose,
and then, with her broad pink tongue,
she licks up one side of my face
and then up the other.

She visits me two nights later.
We lie side by side,
my hand on her paw,
her paw, my hand
the same size.

Between 5:30 and 6:00 a.m.

The crow wings taste a little salty,
like fluted sheets of crunchy nori seaweed.
Only when I'm halfway through one wing
do I realize I could get sick from eating it.
After all, I had found the two on the ground
in that parking lot at the bottom of the steep hill,
the one I had gone down by mistake
having missed the left turn home.

No problem. I'm soon crumbling a brown substance
to make a pie crust before my tennis match
with my colleague Joe, and I'm eager to win.

But instead of Joe,
I encounter a group of Native Americans
playing with toy cars and trucks.
I wonder if I, white and of European descent,
should mention I prefer to be in nature.

Soon Rosie and I are heading out of a harbor
just as the wind picks up,
and we have to swim back
among boats, anchors, and other submerged objects.
A wave washes over her long dog nose
and I reassure her it's alright.

I awake to your whistle,
to a world where I do not munch on crow wings,
a world where we glide into a pure, clear pond,
silhouettes of loons held within glowing early morning mist.

Rosie the Riverer

Dry and serene,
we amble through the pines,
across meadows,
to the bend in the river,
where water carves out swimming holes
and rearranges the shoreline.

Criss-crossing quickly
from one dry rock bed to the other,
over jammed tree trunks,
through fallen brush,
we lean into the river's rush
climbing up and down our legs.

The sky dark, thunder near,
we dive into the deep water,
into a current that carries us
past sandy cliffs,
past bamboo,
toward a tree lying across the river
where, keels unto ourselves,
we slide between the branches,
brushed and blessed by soft green leaves.

I cannot tell you, I really cannot, how happy we are,
rising in the shallows, surrendering to the depths,
but Rosie could, her tail straight up, her eyes gleaming,
and our bodies could, prancing on the sandy shore.

.

Buddha on the Road

I HAVE JUST TURNED OFF ROUTE 2 where it climbs into the hills of Western Massachusetts and follows the
Deerfield River before meandering through the wild
country that borders New York State. Moving slowly over
a dirt-packed side road, I see a little beagle, tail up, on a
spring jaunt, heading straight for the highway.

I'm on my way to my meditation group where
we sit in silence, walk in silence, and discuss the Buddhist
teachings of Thich Nhat Hanh. Right speech. Right liveli-
hood. Right action. I have a few minutes to arrive at that
peaceful little meditation room on time – a few minutes
before the bell sounds and we try to follow our breath and
be in the present moment. But, in this moment, I stop the
car and call to the dog and surprisingly she comes to me. I
tell her to get in and she does. We set off to find her home.

The roads in these hills lead to different worlds. A
few middle-class families live straight ahead in attractive
country homes. I stop to ask if they recognize this dog.
No. They haven't seen her before. I backtrack a couple of
miles and, turning right, I enter a complex of small roads
and houses that remind me of the movie *Deliverance*. Cars
and trucks are parked on lawns. Run-down houses, set
off the road, are slightly ominous. I stop at a house here
and there asking the same question. No, they don't know
her. But then I hit gold. Yes, up the road, a half a mile on
the right, second driveway from the large garden up there

on the hill, there's a bunch of buildings and she lives right there. The house farthest in.

I drive back and forth, never seeing that large garden, asking a few more people. Finally, I ascend a steep driveway and find a man on a second story deck. I receive my final instructions – next driveway on the left. I ask the man what the dog's name is. He thinks a minute, looks down at the dog, looks down at me, and says, "Buddha." Missing meditation, I had found Buddha on the road.

Moments

These are my diamonds:
molten ice in frozen streams
holding clear white light

        Brown oak and beech leaves
        sweep across the first snow,
        last gifts of summer

Sun through pine and fir
spreads like butter through dark kale,
a feast for the soul

        Black crows flying low
        through flakes of falling snow
        glide past my window

Delicate branches,
silhouettes upon the moon,
black strokes of genius

        This pond,
        held in the palm of these hills,
        surrounded by blueberry and pine,
        ripples beneath the great slab of granite
        scraped clean by glaciers
        that once crept across the land.

Thin saplings await
their mother's sweet caresses
when the soft wind blows

This dead porcupine
melting back into the earth
gives such a sweet smell

I cry for the worm
alone at the end of a hook,
bait for her own death

Early morning sun
scatters upon fields of snow,
mirrored jewels of light

Mississippi River

THE MISSISSIPPI EMERGES FROM the end of a beautiful lake in the woods of Northern Minnesota, flowing over rocks, winding its way through grasses and pine trees, clean and clear – and my heart goes out to it.

"Don't go. Don't go. You don't know what you're getting yourself into," I say.

But, of course, it couldn't stop even if it knew it would run past huge cities dumping their endless waste, past power plants, oil refineries, and pesticide-ridden farms.

Ninety-three days down to the Gulf of Mexico. Ninety-three days of carrying boats, carrying garbage. This gentle beautiful creek making soft sounds on a sweet spring morning, heading north before bending south on a journey beyond its imagination.

Free

I HAD BEEN ARRESTED FOR RECEIVING marijuana across international lines and been given two years probation. I reported to my probation officer faithfully every week so they could keep track of me and make sure I wasn't up to breaking more rules. I took the train from Manhattan to Newark, New Jersey and walked through hot dirty streets to a government building to answer questions for a few minutes – a white face in a sea of color.

The opening came in the form of a job offer to type the manuscript of a former professor. She took custody of me, assured them I'd be under her watchful eye, and off we went to Santa Fe, New Mexico. Her daughter and I would go into the surrounding hills and horseback ride through the sage. I was athletic and fearless, so although I had been on a horse only a few times before, I climbed on the horse's back with total confidence. I loved her smell, the softness of her massive muscles so free of tension my hands sunk into them.

We rode bareback under the New Mexican sun, the scent of sage rising as we brushed along the low-lying bushes. Laying low across that broad back, holding onto the mane, I was as free as life itself. This was where I was born to be – in the West on a horse riding across the mesa, like in the Westerns I grew up with and loved so much.

Early one morning, my friend Ruby and I went out to a ranch far from town. "Get into the truck, girls," the ranch hand said. "We'll find the horses where they've been grazing all night." And off we rattled down a dry dusty road until we saw the herd in the distance. The man drove up to the quiet, grazing horses and, saying nothing, he selected two, saddled them up, made sure we were on them, and drove away.

There was a moment when time stopped. No movement, then a bit of restless stirring, then the awakened consciousness that it's feeding time at the barn, and, in an instant, the entire herd with Ruby and I somewhere in the middle took off in a bounding gallop across the mesa. The grass came up to the stirrups. We couldn't see the ground. They say the earth shakes when horses run. The earth shook. They say "the thunder of hooves." The hooves thundered. If we fell off, we were dead, but we stayed on, insignificant in this world of horses. They were free. We were free. Under the open sky, outside of human rule, outside human law.

TWO

FACT AND FICTION

Eduvigis Encarnacion and the Letter 'S'

ONE OF THE MOST DIFFICULT ASPECTS of learning English is actually seeing and then pronouncing the 's' at the end of words. And so it was in my adult English for Speakers of Other Languages, or ESOL, class in the now famous Spring of 2007 when Eduvigis Encarnacion was called upon to read a rather lengthy paragraph in the present tense, a paragraph featuring the adventures of a certain Katie Wong.

Eduvigis (Ed-u-wee-gee) started off slowly as she usually did, having found her place, adjusted her glasses, and stabilized herself with a self-encouraging "Okay" before taking off for destinations unknown. As she stepped one word, a short pause, another word into her reading assignment, I was prepared to repeat a verb or a plural and wait for her to supply the 's' which, to me, seemed to be blinking on and off on the page, jumping up and down, hoping to be recognized and given its rightful place in the pantheon of sounds.

Eduvigis made it through the first, second, third, and fourth sentences pronouncing each word from beginning to end including every 's' strewn in her path. The end of the paragraph was in sight – only four more medium-length sentences to go – and Eduvigis seemed to be teetering on the edge of a world record. I felt myself holding my breath, my eyes widening, the story in my hand gripped tighter, the speed of my heart increasing, as Eduvigis hopped from sentence six to seven before plodding on – one finger leading her eyes across the page.

I have felt this way watching figure skating competitions, important baseball games in the 10th inning, but never in an ESOL class. I was riveted. Was she going to make it? Would she become the one to recognize and give every 's' its due – a feat unparalleled in any class I had ever taught?

The final sentence, rife with "s's", a perfect trap for even the finest verbal athlete, presented itself. Eduvigis heads down the final stretch, her brow furrowed, a study in concentration. I can feel the tension in the room as she meets the next to the last word, the last word, and then crosses the finish line as slowly as she had started, plodding into the annals of English language learning lore – having attained that rarest of achievements.

I burst into applause, laughing in disbelief. I want to drape a gold medal around her neck. Her eyes light up. She relaxes into a broad smile. Here we are, she who had run her own personal marathon, and me, part coach, part Howard Cosell, enthusiastically announcing her triumph to the world.

A Long Way to Go

The Buddhist monks
are creating a mandala,
sifting blue, yellow, red
sand from their hands
to a board on the floor.

Intricate geometric patterns emerge
with a soft hiss
in a crowded room of white middle-class
women, children, and men
sitting cross-legged for hours,
calm, attentive, and present,
in the sun-lit room.

The monks rise, sing and pray.
Silence.
Then in a grand sweeping gesture,
fingers rake through the mandala
and the colors lie
intermingled, formless.

A monk says, "This sand is blessed.
We will carry it to the bridge
and give it to the river where
it will begin its journey to the sea and
bless every being it touches
along the way.

Peace and well-being fill the room.

Then he says, "I have these small
plastic bags and this spoon.
Before we go,
anyone who would like to take
sand home, please stand in line."

The air crackles faintly.
Desire is aroused.
Fear of not getting is aroused.
Trying to appear
calm and non-acquisitive,
people jostle for their
place in line.

All who want receive,
and in procession,
the group walks
into the sunshine
to the bridge.

The monks chant,
the sand is released
to the water
below — the
very few
grains
of sand
left
for
all
the
beings
in
the
watery
path
to
the
sea.

In Yosemite

I WAS ALWAYS AFRAID OF HEIGHTS — ever since I was a kid and a friend said I really could fly and tied wings of hangars and stretched sheets to my shoulders and led me onto the roof and pushed me off the edge. When I hit the ground a profound sense of trust shattered. I couldn't make sense of what had happened and my friend, afraid she had killed me or afraid she hadn't, ran away, having fiercely whispered to me to never tell my mother and we never talked about it again.

All my life, as I stood on the edge of high places, I felt a tingling in my legs and up through my stomach and, although I was on firm ground, I would start to lose my balance and have to say to myself over and over, "It's alright, stay calm," and inch myself backward or along a path until the earth was once more flat before me and no edges were in sight. All that changed the summer my lover, Marina, and I stayed near Yosemite National Park and took the greatest risk we had ever taken in our lives.

Marina had also had a bad experience with heights when her 6-foot-6 cousin held her above his head for 12 hours and 14 minutes in an attempt to enter the Guinness Book of Records for the length of time a person could hold 30 pounds of a living being in the air without taking a break. He held that record for over two years and felt he had made his mark on civilization, but he was totally oblivious to the fact he had also made his mark on Marina. This experience had kept her close to the ground and in control of all physical contact with any other human being for the rest of her life until that day in Yosemite when we threw our pasts away.

Our cabin was about two miles from the edge of an enormous canyon. Every morning for several weeks we had edged our way closer to where the earth suddenly gave way to space and time. When we were within fifty feet, we would both fall to the ground and crawl back until we could no long see the abyss.

But then a strange thing happened. Knowing that the chasm existed, we no longer felt safe even on what appeared to be solid ground. We knew there had once been solid ground where now there was nothing, so why couldn't it happen again – exactly where we were standing?

Whether we were in bed, sitting on a rock outside the cabin, or swimming in a small pond cradled in windswept rock, we were always on edge waiting for the ground to give way. It got so bad that we had no choice but to face our fear or be forever consumed by it, to risk our lives in order to claim them.

We were always a bit extreme – extremely cerebral or extremely physical, extremely combative or extremely conciliatory. Once again, the pendulum swung through our psyches and we moved from extreme fear to bravado and came up with a drastic plan. We would go to the edge and embrace it. We would be still and centered in the face of enormous change and crumbling foundations. I would embrace the void in a symbolic gesture on a rock that jutted out over unimaginable depths and Marina would record this event from a parallel ravine with an old camera that took steady hands and enormous focus.

We practiced for weeks. I balanced on rocks eight to ten feet off the ground while Marina photographed me from logs on small hills. We visualized every moment. We whispered descriptions of space and our calmness in the face of it into each other's ears every night before falling asleep. And then, on July 3rd, on the tenth anniversary of our relationship, we set out to do what had once been impossible for us.

Middle Names

MY PARENTS GAVE ME A LETTER and let me choose my own middle name. I was given B, so, from day one, my initials have been ABC, Amanda B. Collins.

I found a lot of middle names throughout my life that suited me perfectly – like Barbie in grammar school and Baton in high school and Bondage during my heyday in New York City. Then there was Boat during the seventies when I lived on a commune on the coast of Oregon and Blaspheme when I was assistant editor for a magazine that deconstructed American icons.

I named myself Blessed when I had that wonderful lover in the nineties – the one and only – but that changed quickly to Burned when she ran off with the coral reef diver during our vacation in the Bahamas. I never did name myself Bahama though I did love it there and felt I had found my home at last. That incident with the diver though sent me into an existential tailspin during which time I named myself Because. Just because. And then there was But – a name that lasted only a day – given to me by someone I didn't agree with at all and Buttcakes by a fervent admirer.

But now I'm Bad, just plain bad, because my anger is overflowing and I feel like pulling down everything around me. I feel like I'm headed toward choosing Bottomless Pit – though this would be my first time using two words and one of them doesn't even start with a B, though P is about as close to a B as a consonant can get.

Yeah, I'm like some bottomless pit that can't be filled or fill itself, and I don't know what I'm going to do. What am I going to do, ABC? Head down the road toward Buddha, Boundless and Being? Or down that other road to Bitter, Blasted, and Binge? I'm working on it before someone names me Belated. I'm working on it, ABC. I'm working on it.

Ashfield Lake

The lake is frozen.
I cannot swim.
If I took a running start,
I would slide halfway across this lake,
my bathing suit a sled,
my legs and arms its runners.

I feel no resistance,
no rising command
that the lake be the way
I've always known it
all those summers
circling its inner shore
in lazy backstrokes,
my face a landing pad
for dragonflies needing a rest.

There is only amazement
that this place,
at times a liquid bed of lapping waves,
could be so solid
I can walk on water.

I think of you
with your inner landscapes
and mutable weather
and wonder,
how could I ever have thought
to change you?

Gay Bar 2 a.m.

You glide through the darkness of the gay bar
like a white swan on a muddy river.

Tall, blonde, regal,
you float over the sticky floors,
past the female impersonators,
past the gyrating boy in a thong
in the limelight.

You flow across the dance floor
where the booming bass
almost stops our hearts,

where you press your hips, soft breasts
against mine.

Moving Days

You're right.
What emotional irony —
all your friends gathering
to help you move away.

Why don't we refuse?
Have a sit-in right here and now?
Throw our bodies over your towels and shelves
and chant, "Hell no, you can't go!"

Instead, like ants at a crumb fest,
we carry box after box late into the night,
sweat falling from one person onto another.

You move through the chaos
like someone hit over the head,
dreamy-eyed, soft and slow.

I read Buddhist teachings on desire every night,
trying to watch as desire arises,
understand the pain it carries,
acknowledge its endless transformations.
And yet, desire prevails.

I cannot make you stay.

It will be a greater force
that demands a cooling,
or draws us back
into a heat of our own.

An Unlikely Explanation

"This is a test.
Everything is a test,"
you said.
I guess you meant
how well I got along with your children,
our conversations,
how I got along with your friends,
our lovemaking,
how much fun we were having.
I think I did very well.

Then you moved away
and there was a writing test.

I guess I failed,
which is ironic
since I'm an English teacher.

It must have been the content.
I know the grammar was perfect.

Lester

"**H**EY LESTER, YOU FORGOT SOMETHIN'!" she shouted from the collapsing doorway.

"What's that? I got nothin' so how can I forget somethin'?"

"Your teeth, Lester, your teeth. You can't play harmonica without your teeth! Now get on over here and let me fix yuh up!"

"I'm tellin' you, Dora, you don't need no teeth to play harmonica. Fact is, sound's sweeter with no teeth. Breath comes easier, you know that."

But he opened his mouth and she clicked them in and Lester climbed into his truck and took off fast down the road, checking his shirt pockets for the harmonica.

"Least I didn't forget this," he thought, and started to whistle variations on the different tunes he was gonna play. This was an old arrangement with the line dancers at the Thin Line Bar. With not enough people around for a band, the ladies decided they'd play the jukebox and ole Lester would play along givin' the feeling of live music, and this suited him and them just fine.

He pulled up to the door and noticed a crowd was there early. He checked his teeth in the mirror, lowered himself slowly to the asphalt, hitched his pants up, rubbed one boot against his pant leg and then the other, and headed for the door.

"Lester, honey, could you come on over here for a minute?"

The voice was coming from the other side of a pickup truck like it always did. And he walked over, like he always did. And there she was leanin' against the truck bed sayin', "Play me a tune before you go in, Lester."

So he took his harmonica out, wet his lips, and began an old blues song he had learned from a Lightnin' Hopkins record. It was sad and sweet and was carried in the warm air like a sleepy baby in the arms of an angel.

"Now Lester," she said, "come over here." And Lester did.

"Open your mouth, Lester." And he did. And she popped out those teeth. "Now play me another tune, Lester." And he did. And it sounded like the angel herself.

Ce-le-bra-tion Now

I T ALL BEGAN IN AUGUST 2006 WHEN I was observing an English for Speakers of Other Languages class that I was to teach in September. The summer school teacher had planned a lesson on ordinal numbers and each member of the class was reporting on what day of which month they were born. When it was my turn, I said December 14th.

I noticed one student was taking notes. She was around seventy years old, a former gymnast from Russia, with dyed brown hair, substantial makeup, and a lot of energy. The class secretary or social director, I thought briefly, and that was the end of that.

As it turned out, this recorder of data eventually dropped out of the program because she wasn't making any progress in her English skills no matter how long she attended classes. I didn't realize how her limited skills would impact me directly until that October, when, on the 14th, I walked into the classroom after a break, and found the class grinning and singing happy birthday to me. There were presents, cards, food, enthusiasm, pride, generosity. I didn't have it in me to tell them my birthday was not in October, as Galina, it turns out, had recorded.

Okay, I thought to myself, I was born, this is not the exact day, a lot of people celebrate their birthdays on days other than the real one, but maybe I should tell them. No I can't; well, it won't happen again.

Three years passed. Galina dropped out. The students in that class moved on to other teachers or out into the world never to be seen again.

Last week, a student approaches me and whispers, "Marian, it's Luz's birthday. During break can you take her into the hall and keep her occupied?"

"Oh, sure," I say. "I was wondering what was going on."

So Luz and I hang in the hallway while the students remain in the classroom or walk quickly by to heat up some food in the kitchen. A pizza delivery man shows up with the biggest pizza I have ever seen. I coolly direct him to our room as if he shows up every evening.

I'm thinking, wow, Luz is being so good, pretending she doesn't notice the pizza or that her classmates are not talking to her. She knows it's her birthday. She's being so cooperative.

Eventually, a student comes out and tells me to bring Luz in. I walk in fully aware there's going to be a birthday party. I'm clapping and singing *Happy Birthday* with the class as we enter the dark room and then the lights come on and they're singing to me!

There were presents, cards, food, enthusiasm, happiness, pride, generosity. I froze with a surprised grin on my face. What should I do? They're so happy. So convinced. It took so much organizing and money to create this party.

As I'm searching my heart and brain for a good response, someone is putting a party hat on my head. I notice Marcin with two party hats like horns. A "Happy

Birthday" banner is hanging across the board. There's a cake. Homemade food. Everyone is smiling and so pleased with this surprise. Someone is reaching for a camera. I'm being herded over for a class photo. It's mid-October.

I'm hungry. I start eating the pizza. Students are trying to glean some information from me. So you *were* born in October, right? I barely move my head up and down trying not to lie.

Rosa approaches with a card full of cut-out cartoon figures that I am supposed to match with the students in the class. I open it and it blasts, *"Ce-le-bra-tion now, come on!"* Rosa brings the class present and now the cake with my name spelled in red against white within red roses.

Rosa, the one student from that class of three years ago who has remembered and is proudly carrying on the class memory.

Wheel of Fortune

I AM SO SMALL AND THE WORLD IS SO LARGE. I have always been small. Sometimes when I stand up, I can't believe I'm really standing. I'm like that Tim Conway character on *The Carol Burnett Show,* except I'm a nun instead of a golfer. Maybe that's why I turned to God. We are all small but equal before His eyes.

In this human world, I have my ups and downs. I teach second grade at Our Sacred Heart across the street. It's a comfort to be around people smaller than me, but a little embarrassing as my students return taller and taller year after year. I have accommodated by rooting myself firmly in a posture of gratitude and adoration as I view the world from 4-foot-6-inches above the ground. I look up at these expanding children as I look up at Jesus on the cross.

You've caught me in a philosophical moment. I think about life a lot, especially when I watch this program, the *Wheel of Fortune,* which, in my opinion, is one of the most thought-provoking shows on television today. It brings to my consciousness the great Eastern religions, invokes the sense of choice and fate, of cycles being set in motion by the giant hand of God. It makes me think about the repercussions of where we land, what we seem to gain or lose, how we respond. It shows me the enormous energy consumed by the illusion of personal control – the entanglements of joy, grief, regret, and pride – as if one were personally responsible for the outcome of fortune's spinning wheel.

This illusion of control is so powerful. I know because even after all these years of training I sometimes forget that it is God who spins the wheel, who places us strategically for optimal learning, for growing service. The *Wheel of Fortune* reminds me that this is so, and helps me accept my smallness, knowing once again I am the expression of His will, nothing more and nothing less.

Life Lessons Learned
from Doing Crossword Puzzles

≈ If something feels right, it probably is.

≈ If something doesn't feel right, it probably isn't.

≈ If something is not working, try something else.

≈ Commit yourself to accomplishing the task at hand for as long as it takes.

≈ Think big.

≈ Use the governing principle that has been given to you by the Puzzle Maker.

≈ Question what you have.

≈ Let go of a part if it does not help the whole no matter how attached to it you may be.

≈ Allow associations to happen.

≈ Expand your thinking beyond its usual boundaries.

≈ Entertain all possibilities.

≈ Follow hunches.

≈ Trust your intuition.

≈ Approach the problem from different angles.

≈ Work from the simple to the more difficult.

≈ Take chances.

≈ Admit errors.

≈ Recognize every part is essential to the whole.

≈ Know that everything is interconnected.

≈ Look for patterns.

≈ Be open to what emerges.

≈ Delight in the process.

≈ Pick a challenge that stretches but does not defeat you.

≈ Find pleasure in new ways of looking at familiar things.

≈ Have faith that what you know can lead you to finding what you do not know.

≈ Accept that you do not always have all the answers, but rejoice when you do.

≈ When you are stuck, sleep on it and try again in the morning.

≈ Make necessary changes even when the solution is not in sight and you disturb the existing order.

≈ Ask for help when you truly cannot move forward.

≈ Let go of the entire endeavor once you have done all you can and have truly reached your limit.

≈ Learn from what you did not know, so you can do better in the future.

Breath

COLD ARTIC AIR HAS SETTLED OVER NEW ENGLAND. The air that has been drawn into and released from the bodies of the Inuit, the whales, the seals and caribou. The air that has swept over glaciers and wild cold rivers where bears search for food, that has poured over wolves as they sleep pressed against each other, as they run for their lives from hunters in helicopters. This wild air has settled over crowded New England towns and cities, over the open land percolating with interwoven life. This air that makes its way into my body and out into the world again.

On one of these cold mornings, I am walking through the pine forest that stands above the Green River. This is a particularly beautiful forest that takes my breath away whenever I enter and see the light settled on the trunks and dancing off the dangling fingers of leaves. Standing in the slanting rays of a rising sun, I sigh and see my breath travel to the nearest tree and gently rub up against its bark. My next breath is held in the light and particles of color like painted atoms spread before disappearing into the cold air. It is amazing how far one's breath can go. How completely it vanishes. How inexorably it will be taken in by another. I wonder. Does a sigh of sadness carry sadness? A sigh of joy carry joy?

Back on the frozen seat of my car, my breath freezes on the inside of the windshield. Feeding the birds that snowy morning, I cannot see their breath. Watching the playoffs, I see pockets of breath in front of the players' faces like little white clouds suspended before buffalo on the plains.

Indoors, with unknown others, I become very conscious that the air I take in is the air they have let out and sometimes I hesitate and breathe shallowly. But with you, when we sit, when we lie nose to nose, I draw your breath deep inside where it mingles with mine and the breath of the fox, the beaver, the coyote.

THREE

FAMILY

Gathering Speed

ONE SUMMER, A LONG TIME AGO, my family went on vacation in the hills of Pennsylvania. On a beautiful afternoon, my sister Morgan, my father and I walked to the top of a long hill. We then left the dirt road and walked through cow fields where Morgan and I lay down and started rolling through the pasture. I rolled and rolled, eventually stopping and watching the world spin around me. I slowly became conscious of my sister shouting in the distance. She was screaming, "I can't stop! I can't stop! I can't stop!"

I sat up and saw her still rotating, gathering speed, bouncing off of small outcroppings, spinning out of control down the hill. I leapt up, ran as fast as I could and lay down in her path. She hurtled towards me. I braced myself for contact. I felt her hit my left side, roll over me and continue, but her speed was broken and she rolled slowly to a stop.

Many years later, my other sister, Liz, did not spin, but actually slid out of control in Massachusetts. She, her young daughter Julie, and I were walking along a country road when we saw a long, snowy hillside, covered with a sheet of ice. First Julie took a running leap and slid about one-third of the way down the hill. Then I took off and came to a natural stop near her. Then Liz took off and once again, I saw a sister gathering speed. She whizzed towards us, shrieking, "I can't stop! I can't stop!" Julie and I braced ourselves and with exquisite timing grabbed her as she shot between us. I couldn't figure this out. Was this a hereditary characteristic? Was I going to manifest it someday?

As time went on, however, I saw that this tendency existed outside of my family. My friend Sylvia also gathered speed, but, in her case, she actually disappeared. We were traveling cross-country. She was in her late forties and looking for a commune to settle down in and I was her driver. We stopped at a campground and took a walk up a hill. It seemed safe enough. But coming down, Sylvia started to move a little peculiarly. Her body appeared to be ahead of her feet. Her feet were trying to catch up with her body. Little clouds of dust formed behind her. She was heading for the trees where the path seemed to suddenly end. I was worried; there was no way I could stop her. I saw her grasp wildly at the air, and then, in a moment of athletic splendor, she grabbed a rope hanging from one of the trees, swung into space, and was gone. When I reached her, she was seated on a pile of leaves, looking up, dazed.

What does this mean, this phenomenon of hurtling women? When walking with family and friends, should I warn them or just place myself in a strategic position, eternally vigilant for another gravitational dance?

American Made

MY FATHER WAS A UNION ORGANIZER and every two years he would trade in his car for another American-made model. He bought a white and aquamarine Henry J and a Ford Fairlane, a perfect picnic table for my sister and I as we sat in the open windows and spread our food on the roof. He bought an Edsel which, it turned out, was unsafe because the engine could burst into flames upon impact, and he bought the Corvair which was brought back home after he had been found dead under mysterious circumstances.

I remember the smells of those new cars – full of chemicals, full of promise, full of the mystery of where we would go in them. My father used to take us, his daughters, for rides on the weekends – to Coney Island to swim in the ocean and walk the boardwalk, to Chinatown to pick up Chinese food, a local airport to watch planes land, and Eagle Rock where we'd race across the fields. Once we went to his union office where we were told to wait in a musty wooden meeting hall while he disappeared into the cavernous, quiet, and empty building. Perhaps he was going to do some work, perhaps he was meeting the woman he was having an affair with. Who knew?

Who knew where he went when emotional life in our family got rough and he simply walked out the door, got in his American-made car, and drove off? Or where he went early in the morning after telling us a company was on strike? Maybe he actually went to the picket line, day after day, month after month, year after year.

Who knew where his American-made car had taken him before he coasted into the driveway late at night and stopped beneath our bedroom window – the sound of the engine in the silence of the night, the car door closing, and his footsteps leading him into the American-made family he couldn't trade in, no matter how much he wanted to do just that.

Ping Pong

MY FATHER BUILT A PING PONG TABLE when my sisters and I were children. Perhaps because he wasn't athletic by any stretch of the imagination and had no interest in sports whatsoever, it never occurred to him that there was an official table size, that there were standard measurements of any kind for sports equipment. He must have contemplated what a ping pong table should look like or perhaps a friend was getting rid of wood or perhaps he found it, but somehow we ended up with an enormous table set on wooden horses with an official net strung across the middle.

My sisters and I played ping pong a lot. It wasn't until we were older and out in the world that we came across other ping pong tables, and they seemed so small. Whenever we went for a slam or a nick off the end or any other move guaranteed not to be returned, the ball would miss the table by inches.

Looking back I see this as a perfect example of our upbringing. We were brought up with values and in situations that bore no relationship to standard society. Through time we have managed to play the game to some degree, but we usually land somewhere outside the boundary of regulation-size behavior.

Secrets

H E HAD A SECRET, A BIG SECRET, and though he never told his children, we knew what it was, knew we had to keep it. If not, he might be taken away, put in jail, maybe, we believed, even killed.

It was the 1950s and we were in elementary school. Our mother had told us never to reveal that our father was a union organizer. The McCarthy hearings were in full swing and Communists were being hauled in front of the televised investigations of the House of Un-American Activities Committee. From all the warnings and bits of information over the years, it was not hard to conclude that our father could be considered one of these enemies of the State.

The FBI had been coming around sporadically, prowlers in a small suburban neighborhood. The agents, caricatures of themselves in trench coats and brimmed hats, had found a link to our family through a next door neighbor who reported my parents' schedules and listened in on our party line.

It was no surprise, therefore, that thirty-five years later, my sister Morgan and I could consider that her co-worker was actually seeing faces of spies in her TV set and in points of light on her bedroom walls. It was the summer of 1990 when the telephone rang in the early evening.

"A friend from work is coming over," Morgan said. "There's something she wants to tell me that she can only say in person." Fifteen minutes later, there was knock on the door and Morgan was taken away into the night up into the nearby mountains. Two hours later she returned, visibly shaken.

"Something strange is going on. She says that people from work are suspicious of her and have infiltrated her house. When she watches TV, she sees their faces behind the screen and she goes up to pinpoints of lights on her walls and sees their tiny faces looking at her. Do you think it's possible?"

I wasn't sure. Chills had run up my spine as she told me this, especially when I pictured the possibilities being whispered on a dark mountain road out of range of suspected high-tech listening devices. Familiar images of FBI agents, stool pigeons, and wiretapping emerged and, at first, it did seem possible. Technology had come a long way since the fifties and maybe now they could do such things.

It was only by conscious acts of will that we were able to take shaky steps toward the concept that no, it probably wasn't true, it didn't seem possible. Over a couple of days, my sister and I came to the decision – a correct one as it turned out – that the woman was on drugs and having paranoid fantasies. But coming to this conclusion took a will power that only other red diaper babies would truly understand.

Mom's Miracles

YOU LAY IN THE MIDDLE OF THE BED in the nursing home, so small, moving in and out of memory, absorbed moment by moment in what you were seeing on the ceiling or coming through the empty door. Once you murmured you were afraid to die, but only once, and by the time we had deciphered your words, you had been carried away by another thought.

How you wanted to see your father, the love of your life. Your father, the man you kept your eyes on, so you seemed to be walking backwards through life ever since 1925, the year he suddenly died. But even that longing for him did not lead you to believe in life after death where you could finally see him again. When we offered you that hope, you said, "I don't believe in it. Do you?" And when we replied, "Anything is possible," you answered, "Well, when *you* get to Heaven, say hello to him for me."

I wonder, though, how do you explain this? The photograph of his handsome face, as large as life, hanging on the wall across from the foot of your bed. Between you and him a vase of flowers and, as the hour of your death approaches, the flowers vibrating. Only those flowers. Nothing else in the room. And as you start to take your last breaths, we are singing that verse in Amazing Grace, "When this flesh and heart shall fail and mortal life shall cease, amazing grace shall then prevail in heaven's joy and peace."

And this. Although you were not religious, the women of the temple are summoned and the next day you are prepared for the ritual bathing of the dead. I visit you that morning and brush a fly from your forehead and you do not move. I kiss your forehead and feel how cold you are and see you aren't shivering. Your face is tense, worried, mouth slightly open. You are dressed in white muslin with a white muslin hood. I go outside and speak to the washers of the dead and then wait.

The women wash your body while reciting a prayer forgiving all sins. You are sent from this life clean and free from the weight of wrong choice and wrong action. You are dead, frozen, and yet, when I see you again, your face is relaxed, so peaceful, so serene.

I know that somewhere in you, you knew you had sometimes done wrong though you never took responsibility or sought redemption. But somehow, in death, you responded to forgiveness. And, if that is possible, perhaps you *are* with your father, and, if you are, say hello to him for me.

Ashes to Ashes

After the cleansing ceremony, my mother's body was sent away to be cremated, and a week or two later, my sister and I returned to the funeral home to pick her up. My first reaction upon seeing the box that held her was *it's so small*. This person in whose watery body I had swum, who was larger-than-life, was now dry, gray, granule, contained.

We kept her ashes until her memorial service. We kept them as we contemplated her gravestone. My sisters and I had long conversations about what seemed essential about our mother, Lottie, and then we found an engraver who manifested our ideas.

At the top of the horizontal gravestone were the first bars of Beethoven's *Ode to Joy*. Lottie had loved classical music and opera. Under the notes were her name and the dates she had arrived and left this earth. Beneath that was Daughter of Aaron — no mention of her mother, her husband, her children — for all of us were microscopic in terms of the emotional space we occupied when compared with the vast sun of her father whom she hadn't actually seen for seventy-five years.

Below Daughter of Aaron, we quoted her: *It's all in your attitude!* She had written that on a piece of paper which she had put on her refrigerator in Philadelphia after she returned to her birthplace at the age of sixty-five, a mythic journey from a restless, unfulfilling, emotionally cold life in the New Jersey suburbs to the vibrant, culture and friend-filled life she created for herself in the City of Brotherly Love. After this move, Lottie became a mother and advisor. She was living proof that indeed it is all in your attitude.

So we had that engraved and ended her proclamation with an exclamation point in the form of an ice cream cone. The engraver wasn't used to drawing ice cream cones on gravestones, but we insisted, knowing that ice cream was among the great loves of her life, along with her father, music, Philadelphia, and a good laugh – though not necessarily in that order.

On the morning we carried her ashes to the old Jewish cemetery on the outskirts of Philadelphia, we walked through the same black iron gates our family had walked through forty-one years before when we had gathered to bury her mother. That was the only familiar landmark as we made our way to her open grave where we played opera on a cassette player and took the plug from the bottom of the urn so she could return to the ground of her beloved city.

We took some of her ashes and searched for her father's grave. None of the gravestones looked like hers. Most were old and in Hebrew, but we found Aaron, and sprinkled some of her ashes on his grave so she could be reunited at last with the man who shared our lives as much as if his physical body had been with us all those years.

Now some of my mother's ashes are helping the lilac and rose bushes and daffodils grow in our gardens.

Now the ashes of Pilar, my dog, are in a beautiful case in my house beneath a statue of Buddha. And the small tin of my cat's ashes, Miles' ashes, receives the first light on the windowsill among the plants as the sun rises.

And someday my ashes, mixed with those of my beloved animal family, will blow around Whitton Pond, all of us watery creatures dry as bone finding our ways home.

Smaller and Smaller

My mother and her sisters were small.
As time went by, they became so small that objects,
like a bathroom sink or the inside of a car,
seemed drastically out of proportion.

Images from *The Incredible Shrinking Woman*
came to mind, though it never got to the point
where they had to stand on a kitchen counter
to pull their food onto a pan
or live in a dollhouse.

They stood together,
reminiscent of a newly-cropped low hedge.
I once felt I towered above them.

As I grow older,
that is no longer the case.
I too am returning to the earth,
not toppling like a giant redwood,
but melting,
as they once did,
downward,
inward.

Flying

The river is wide,
the deep running water puckering
in small dark, small waves.

Surrounded by flat open space,
small rocks here and there,
I run, and at the river's edge,
leap high,
arms and legs waving,
as I fly over this vast river
into the open arms of my soft round grandmother
waiting for me
on the steppes of Russia.

I have always flown alone,
until last night,
when we were gliding
naked and spooning
a few inches above a city sidewalk
as people walked by
blessing our love
with their smiles.

What Each Day Brings

DRIVING HOME, I FEEL THE DAY lying before me empty as a seashell sky. I decide to buy celery and walk into a store. Its wooden floors hold the smell of territories claimed by cats in the night while customers sleep and mice try to get a decent meal. The air is heavy, the produce wilting, and that first deep breath outside a gift from the gods.

Down the street I see a group of women sitting around a table. A workshop is beginning and an invisible line reels me in and the workshop begins. Music wafts through our open air tent and I bounce in my seat, bounce a lot, smiling and laughing, and the women around me are bouncing too.

The leader gives us an assignment. The directions are simple: go into the university right behind us. And that is when I meet Irv, my uncle Irv, who died of a heart attack while singing a folk song on stage at a Catskill resort. Uncle Irv, our family's Willie Loman, who sold steak knives and ladies' underwear, and was always restless and losing his job. A big man – tall, overweight, balding, clean and neat like men were in the fifties – with a small guitar that lay like a baby against his chest.

I am so happy to see him. With a pomegranate in hand, I gesture does he want some. He nods yes and sits on the university steps and I sit at his feet and place one red jewel after another in his palm. We're grinning at each other, not speaking a word, as I place more and more kernels in his open hand.

Suddenly we're in a classroom and he's the teacher. He starts to write on the board, but the letters turn quickly into drawings: a man running, dashing with a rifle with smoke coming out of the barrel. Then the man's face becomes the face of the North Wind, strong and gentle, and through his white beard comes the breath that blows all the smoke away.

Now I'm in another classroom with another teacher, a small mid-Eastern man, and the students are all men. The teacher's ideas and style are very interesting until he says, "except Jews," and I challenge him until he has no intellectual option but to include Jews. Most of the class gets up and leaves, but I'm disappointed, having really enjoyed the discussion and all that thinking.

I had been listening to Byron Katie before sleeping, listening to her urging us to be in the moment, to not relive the same character in the same story over and over for a lifetime. Sitting here with friends, talking about creating one's life, about honoring ancestors, about teachers and teaching styles, has brought me back to my dream and the eagerness to see what each day brings — to not head home for protection on a seashell morning, but into the world to see what happens.

In the Womb

THE WOMB WAS VERY LUXURIOUS, very spacious at the beginning, but as my twin sister and I grew over the months, we filled what space there was until neither of us could move at all.

My mother, a small woman, held big babies: eight pounds six ounces and six pounds four ounces. But who knew? Before our birth, people just knew we were large enough to create a table out of my mother's stomach, a table so large she could eat her meals from a plate that lay flat upon it.

Many years later, my sister was hypnotized and traveled back into the womb. She remembered the moment I was born. How her world suddenly filled with space. How she reached out her tiny hands and stretched her baby body. She had twenty minutes to herself before swimming out with a smile on her face.

Our Vacation

I T IS THE SUMMER OF 1983. My twin sister Morgan and I haven't spent any significant time alone really ever, so we decide to take a vacation together. She is living in Maine. I'm marooned on the island of Manhattan. Camping on an island off the coast of Maine sounds perfect.

Morgan is in charge of the plans. She has heard about camping on gorgeous Isle au Haute – how easy it is to get to, to camp on, to make boat reservations now that it is off-season.

Since the boat would be leaving us about 500 yards from the campsite, we shop for food with abandon. Canned goods, bags of granola, bags of apples – whatever catches our eyes. This is fun already. Then come the sleeping bags, flashlights, changes of clothes, and a new water bag to keep at our campsite – for a leisurely shower after a gentle swim perhaps.

After unloading at the pier of a very small village, we enter a tiny grocery store to inquire about which footpath to take to our reserved site. "Oh," the woman says. "The campground is on the other side of the island. The boats stopped running there last week."

We are young. We are strong. We are ignorant. We have a map. *Well, it doesn't look that far.* So, I strap one bag to the front of me and balance it with another on my back and grab a grocery bag in each hand. Morgan loads herself down and then we set off, like two pack mules, down a small trail. It is ten in the morning.

I still have pictures of that first journey. Me sprawled on the ground with what appears to be all my worldly possessions sprayed around me. Morgan trying to catch her breath, limp on the ground, held up by a tree trunk. But we do make it, just before dark, with just enough time to make our beds and for me to run a quarter mile back down the trail with the new canvas water bag to get some water.

This is so cool, I think, feeling very proud we have prepared so well for our needs. I fill the bag. The water is very heavy. But I notice in the dimming light that my load is feeling lighter little by little and, by the time I get back to the campground, it is actually manageable, almost all of the water, it turns out, having dripped out on the bag's maiden voyage.

The next morning we awake optimistic and adventurous. We decide to eat as much as possible to lighten our load. We look at the map. *Hmmm. This loop looks pretty short. We'll explore and then just hang out.* Nine hours later, we stumble back to camp just as it is getting dark and fall into our sleeping bags. *Okay. We're getting a feel for the scale of the map and the terrain of the island.*

The next day we prepare for what seems like a reasonable walk. We eat a lot for breakfast and then head for a cove where Morgan has heard there are mussels we can gather and boil. We leave with a pot and sterno can and, at the last minute, I grab a huge box of wooden matches to start the fire.

We walk and walk, swim and walk and walk, and walk, getting hungrier and hungrier, until we finally arrive ravenous at the cove in the early afternoon. We collect a potful of mussels and immerse them in sea water and huddle behind some large rocks to get out of the brisk wind that has just picked up. Firmly securing the sterno in a crevice and balancing the pot on rocks around it, we open the box of matches. There are two – two! – matches rattling around in that big space. Two chances to eat. Two. Chances.

The first match, struck, doesn't catch and wears down. We look at each other. Hold our breath. The second match. The second match catches. The breeze is blowing. We protect the flame with cupped hands. The sterno catches the flame! We eat.

Then Morgan says, "I heard there was a red tide around here recently." We look at each other. We lie down and wait to die. Not a bad place to die. Sort of peaceful. The waves lapping near our feet. The white clouds beautiful against the clear, blue sky. The sound of seagulls in the air. We had come into the world together and perhaps now it is time to leave together. We wait and wait, we're alright. Time to head back.

Let's go this way. It hugs the shoreline. We can't get lost. And so we walk, joyful we've survived our lunch. The temperature is perfect. The air luminous. After a couple hours, we come to a chasm and photograph our shadows in petroglyph postures projected onto the rock cliff across from us. *Hmmm.* *Across from us: dark shadows. The sun's going down! Chasm! Beach far below! Hey, here's a hole in the brush! We can't go back! We've gotta try it!*

I lie on my stomach and inch my way in with Morgan close behind. We slide down the rabbit hole. Slowly at first, then quickly, and finally reach the beach. We start running. No flashlights. Up a hill, over rocks. And, just as it's getting dark, we stumble into our campsite, into our sleeping bags, in wonder at the vastness of the island, the smallness of our map.

The next day we pack up and walk back across the island to catch our boat home. We think maybe we should start a travel agency called ETU: Expect the Unexpected. This turns out to be prophetic, for as the years go by, we find ourselves hiking inland as hikers are running out ahead of severe thunderstorms, we swim in a hurricane, we arrive in the Everglades at dusk with no place to sleep.

Hey, Morgan! Where do you want to go next?

Halloween Wedding in Vermont

"WAIT A MINUTE!" MY SISTER SHOUTS. "I have to trim my beard!"

"But I need the scissors. You've had them all day."

Bernice is not involved. She is quiet, contemplating the front of a one dollar bill. "How's my hair? Does this look right?"

I myself hadn't realized that George's hair was so flat on top. I thought it puffed up which is why I suggested Washington to her in the first place. His flat top with hair curled under by the ears was a bit unattractive.

"Maybe you need to cut some hair on the sides," I mumble, pressing a black beard along my jaw line with two-sided tape.

Meanwhile, on the other side of town, Gandhi has just finished pinning her diaper and winding a sheet around her body after her partner has glued a gray and black moustache of admirable quality to her upper lip. And in Burlington, two Black Panthers grab their dime store rifles and head for the door. The Hare Krishnas are already in character, bobbing and blessing, while Eleanor Roosevelt adjusts her hat and takes the arm of Amelia Earhart.

One of the brides, tall, hefty, always seen in pants and a shirt, is squeezing herself into a black cocktail dress, moussing her hair, and applying glittering eyelashes and makeup. She would later report that her cleavage, rarely seen in public, was a like another person in the room.

The other bride, small, feminine, and strong, dons her black cap, bright pink stockings, loose jacket and orange tie and they head out to greet their guests, all eighty of us.

Inside the bar, the potluck table is filling with stuffed mushrooms, California rolls, salads, cheeses, breads, dips, and spanikopita, and the bar is hopping with historical figures trading in their complimentary tickets for wine. History kaleidoscopes through the room as guests greet each other, talking and laughing with delight.

And then the lights of the room dim as tiny white and orange lights luminate an arched trellis and Pachelbel's *Canon* fills the room. The bridal couple, together twenty years, glide elegantly though the crowd as drag queen and Stonewaller to the enthusiastic roar of family, friends, and coworkers. And soon, Justice Brandeis, aka their twenty-two-year-old son, invested by the State for the day with the power to legally officiate, marries them.

The ceremony is brief and the toasts begin. My sister, as Vincent van Gogh, acknowledges the special relationships between siblings, such as the one Vincent had with his brother Theo, and the one my sister shares with the bride. Abe Lincoln talks about being proud to be in the 21st century when rights are being extended to all people who love each other. And when the dancing begins, Prince boogies with Pete Seeger, a Beatle dances with a local carrot, Abe dances with George, Eleanor dances with Gandhi. . . .

I have often wondered why fighting for equality in marriage and the military, two conventional pillars of straight society, are at the top of the official gay agenda. I have hoped that gay people would not be just like straight people, but really shake things up. This wedding, an incredible twist on a time-honored tradition, showed me this may, in fact, be possible.

FOUR

INNER WORLD

My Best Comeback Ever

"Is that confetti?" she asked,
gazing at the forkful of alfalfa sprouts
heading toward my mouth.

"Yes," I said, "it is.
I'm celebrating my inner life."

Waiting for Test Results

THE DOCTOR'S OFFICE CALLED AT 10:51 A.M. "This is Jan. Please call as soon as possible."

It is now 8:30 p.m. and I'm leaving work. Panic sets in immediately. I had gotten blood work done at 10:30 a.m. the day before. The only possible reason the doctor's office would be calling within twenty-four hours is because there is something wrong, terribly wrong, that has to be addressed immediately. It can't even wait until my appointment next week.

The scenarios come fast and furious. They had done a routine AIDS test that I didn't know about and it came back positive. My hypothyroidism had become so haywire, they were strongly suspecting a tumor on my pituitary gland. But now I can't have a brain scan because I have a metal plate in my arm! Well, right before the arm surgery, my red and white blood cell count was really good. Excellent platelet numbers too. Could so much have gone so wrong in those two and a half months? Leukemia. I have been feeling tired lately.

I get home and try to calm myself. Tea. A little Buddhist philosophy. I fall asleep. At 3:00 a.m. I'm wide awake. I troll my mind looking for comforting words from Eckhardt Tolle. Yes, I remember. Don't identify with your illness. Nothing is permanent. Stay in the moment. Everything changes. I'm glad I remember that part.

Then *Tricycle* magazine. I turn the pages and see someone in robes with a shaven head. I can't tell at first if this is a woman or a man. The face is not conventionally good-looking, but I stay with it, following the contours. The nose goes a bit this way, the mouth a bit that way. She's wearing rimless glasses and I can see her eyes so clearly. They are looking at me with kindness, with love, and are truly beautiful. I lay her picture across my chest and fall asleep.

I call the doctor at 8:00 a.m. No one is available. I've got to get out of the house. I need air. I walk down the deserted sunlit streets and up Smead Hill Road to where I see miles of green pine-covered hills rolling east. Only a few houses are visible in the early morning light. This is where I sleep, I think. In this vast forest under a vast sky.

My head is full of me, my fears, my fantasies. I am huge to myself. My personal universe fills all the space until I picture myself on that far-off hill, a pinpoint I could never identify. Tiny, tiny, little me in this vastness. Tiny, tiny, little every one whirling in their own huge, transient worlds within a universe cradling us all.

I'm feeling calmer now. Okay, I need to face the bad news. But, how do I know it's really bad. I've heard people say that their illness was the best thing that had ever happened to them. They get kicked out of their ruts. They appreciate each moment. Maybe I'll meet someone, someone in my medically appropriate support group, and have a great relationship. How do I know what's good or bad?

There's no return message on my answering machine. On the way to my sister's, I realize it's good I'll be with family when I get the news. My sister tends to play down medical problems, so she'll help keep me calm, and my niece will try to be positive too.

Once there, I call my answering machine. The nurse has left a message. The test results look fine, she said, but we didn't order one of them. We're calling to find out who did.

.

The Battle is Over

These pines, swaying seaweed,
these birds, darting fish,
me, a barnacle
determined to stay attached to the Now.

I am not letting my mind,
always looking for trouble,
always looking for trouble,
to go anywhere
but deeper into Here.

I remember that dendrite,
the one in the nature film,
rising from its habitual connection
because the order to fire,
again and again,
in that exact way,
had stopped.

I am no longer firing
those endless volleys of regret,
of self-recrimination.

The battle is over.
There are no dead,
only us
under the eclipsing moon
watching the changing light.

Release

Snow has fallen in the forest.
Branches of hemlock are pressed to the ground
held by a weight they cannot lift alone.
They are still.
They wait beneath flakes of snow,
so light when they fell,
so heavy when welded
storm after storm.

Now the sun is returning north,
drawing the snow like magic
into the warming days.
The balance shifts.
The branches bounce into the air
spraying the last remnants of snow
back into their original lightness.

I long for such a moment
in my own life.

The Sweatshop is Closed

We, the worker slave cells of your mind,
do hereby declare the revolution has begun.

It will end only when you open your eyes
and let the light wash through this dark factory,
only when these patterns we have been forced to reproduce
day after day, year after year,
melt into formlessness in the heat of change.

Locked too long into black and white,
we now honor our gray matter,
which holds both black and white,
which hold all the colors of this world.

The sweatshop is closed.
The art studio is open.

The revolution has begun.

Footprints

She had wailed her way through the woods
the day before,
calling out to the sky
like Job reborn,
like tribal women at a funeral.

Her footsteps are encrusted in the snow,
fossilized tracks of a primitive animal in ancient mud,
toes pointed slightly outward,
steps processional,
the sounds of her chains hanging in the air
low to the ground.

Here she is again
on another beautiful day,
settled and clear,
yet unwilling to place her feet in her own footprints,
unwilling to pick up that despair through her soles.

Now she strolls beside her previous self,
a witness, a companion,
no longer the one who would set her feet down
in that exact way
again.

Darkness

I am walking in darkness,
feeling the walls of this labyrinth,
sweating in fear of being lost.

I didn't prepare.
I have no light strapped to my forehead,
no map,
no compass,
no line out.

I try to remember the paths
that brought me here.

I see that at every turn
I chose the smaller space,
the dimmer light.

I awaken now
to a deeper fear,
not of being lost in this darkness
but of being exposed
in the light.

Sleep

I was disappointed
when I discovered
I could not lose myself
in sleep anymore,

that sleep grew tired of itself
and needed a rest.

Delirium

I must be reaching the end of this tissue box
after all this gagging up of lost battles,
this expulsion of detritus
that reappears as soon as it's collected.
I vow not to buy any more.

I will let the fallen
seep down my face,
cast me into a monument
to their willingness to die
for my life.

I will no longer bury the dead in soft white coffins,
but infuse this battlefield
with a thousand blessings,
a thousand invitations to heal.

Change

I was chugging down a track
through a land I knew.

The markers, hammered into the ground
at predictable intervals,
did not tremble in the wind.

The soot of the engine,
seeping over the cars,
sliding through window cracks,
settled over the seats and narrow aisles
as the world went by.

This train was going somewhere,
and hitched to its ambitions
I was lulled by the rhythms of its elliptical gears,
and the sound of metal rolling effortlessly over metal.

The switchman in the railroad yard had other plans.
In the quiet of the night,
pulling this rod, yanking that rope,
he sent my car gliding
through sheer momentum
down a side track
to a stunned,
silent
halt.

Now I leave this car
and step onto the tracks,
naked as a snail's body reaching
into dark, moist-laden air.

Personal Passport

I am an animal on planet Earth,
my place of origin unknown,
composed of cosmic dust,
age approximately 40,000,000,060.

My place of birth is each moment,
my country, the land of rivers and trees.

I declare to all who wish to listen
that all beings are equal.

Here is my life, my passport
from this life to the next,
stamped with what I have given,
what I have taken away.

Wisdom Way Transfer Station

Today I have come to this sky
where I always feel at peace,
the sky atop a hill outside my town,
the sky above the transfer station
where people come to bury what they no longer need.

I have come to write in the company of the discarded,
in the company of things to be transformed,
where citizens, in ritual procession,
lay down the weight of their lives.

There is sacredness in the sky here,
in the receiving ground,
in the workers carrying the unwanted
toward transmutation, resurrection.

Floating Through the World

I enter the town co-op and wander to
my place at the end of the counter
where I bag groceries in my little green apron,
a cipher in a complex moving jigsaw puzzle
whose picture reflects no part of me.

Forlorn, tight, enclosed,
I bag until a man with tortoise shell glasses,
a clean white ironed shirt and modest pants,
glides past the cashier to retrieve his food
at the end of the line.

He reaches for the bag.
He stops.
He looks into my eyes.
With great focus and total attention,
he commands, "Have a good week."

I have been thinking of that moment of being seen,
how it suffused me,
how it brought me to the place where I could see again.

Could see that little worm that afternoon
on the path by the river,
covered in sand, breaded and drying,
tiny under the open sky.
The worm I picked up, washed off,
and placed gently in the moist grass.

Containers

I.

THE ROOM AT THE RADIO STATION IS SMALL, square, and dim. A fan blows air in from the adjoining room. One would not know there is an outside world, that the sun is shining. This room has two ways out: the door, and the microphone, a magic tunnel to the ears of drivers and people at home skimming their radio dials.

Yesterday I was such a person, driving in my car, when I remembered the station was replaying my show that very moment, and sure enough, there were the songs I had chosen, and then my voice coming back to me as I reviewed Obama and McCain's records on the environment, expressing my incredulity that someone could actually vote against clean water and clean air.

"McCain breathes, doesn't he?" I ask. "He and his family drink water! Why wouldn't he vote for clean air and water based on that alone?"

Good point, I think, parked in front of the Big Y, fascinated with myself coming through the speakers.

II.

I had been thinking about defined spaces having heard Pema Chodron the other night describe how the container of her vow of celibacy allowed her the freedom to glow with sexual energy, knowing she would never act on it. She reminded me of the Buddhist teaching that meditation brings practitioners to the edge of their thought-defined containers which then shatter, leaving them in a larger space whose edges, in time, will also fall.

III.

Now I'm sitting here, in the container of this house, my writing a morphed microphone, having just driven past the lake on a gray fall morning. The sky lies low, darker than the earth. The golden yellow of the fallen maple leaves is the sun today – glowing from the ground, filling my eyes and mind with a light so strong, it radiates me out of my small life into a beauty so vast, I cannot imagine its boundaries.

Ruminations on Getting Old

I KEEP THINKING IF I HAVE A GOOD NIGHT'S SLEEP and take a hot shower, I'll look the way I did ten years ago. It doesn't work. I catch a glimpse of myself in a store window and think, *I don't remember being so small, and my head, especially from the right, looks like an ancient turtle.* And when I lie down, my once muscular body looks so soft, with ripples of mysterious, alien body matter. Once in a while I catch a glimpse of my former self when the conditions are right, which usually include a dimness of light and an imperfect reflective surface.

I now realize all the me's that have lived up to this moment have died. The me who ran fast through the woods, sidestepping rocks, leaping over crevasses. The me who leapt into the air to catch a ball. The me who was so fixated on intimate relationships. Now I sometimes understand the Buddhist advice to die to each moment. Then, at the end of life, there is only that last moment to lose and not a lifetime.

When young, I thought that people were born old though I was told that the old were once young. I even saw pictures of them young, but I never really believed it. Now I know how consistent the spirit is and how it resides barely changed in old bodies. Now, when I see someone old, I visualize how they looked at twenty or ten. I look at young people and imagine how they'll look at sixty or seventy. How that forward thrust of the head will become permanent, how those eyes will recede under bushy eyebrows. They don't know this will happen, just like I didn't.

I remember a photograph of the face of an elegant woman artist. Her head is shaved, her face has no expression. She is looking straight into the camera. She is at least eighty years old. Every wrinkle is etched as deeply and clearly as ravines seen from the air. And then I imagine her face after the shutter clicks, the life force flowing freely into those ravines, all obstacles removed by her willingness to see, be seen, to be.

FIVE

POLITICS

A Dream

The radio is on.
I hear the voice of an expert
on National Public Radio
articulating United States policy,
outlining possible,
but unlikely,
solutions in Iraq.

Meanwhile,
Les from the
International Education Office
at my school
is doing a hip-hop dance
in an animal suit.
A group of Iraqi children,
are smiling and clapping,
delighted.

Tompkins Square Park

NEW YORK CITY. THE EAST VILLAGE in the late 60s. Young middle-class hippies are moving in displacing poorer Hispanics and other ethnic groups. Tompkins Square Park. Smack in the middle. A place where cultures move like rivulets of oil through water.

It's a warm summer morning and the city air moves lazily through the streets. I leave my sister's apartment — the one with the bathtub in the kitchen, the rent sixty-five dollars a month — and head for the park.

Finding a secluded spot, I sit on the ground with my back against a brick wall and start reading Ralph Ellison's *Invisible Man*. This is nice — sitting in the dappled sunlight, away from the traffic, the strangers on the sidewalk, the apartment that holds the smells, the lives of generations.

Splat. A rotten apple smashes into my arm. A grinning Hispanic boy is peering at me over a high fence, very pleased with the accuracy of his aim, with his victorious encounter with the enemy. To this boy's amazement, I take what's left of the apple, spring to my feet, and sprint after him until I throw the apple as hard as I can and hit him square in the middle of his back.

Hmmm, I think, time to get out of here and I start walking slowly toward the park exit. Soon I see a gang, ranging in age from early teens to early twenties, approaching from behind, and I recognize the boy leading them directly towards me. Wham! I'm whacked on the back of my head. They've sent their toughest girl to take me on, to retrieve the boy's dignity by taking this hippie girl down.

"I don't want to fight," I say and keep walking, but the girl jumps on my back and the rumble begins. I pin her to the ground and hold her arms over her head. I look up at the faces of the boys hovering in a circle over us.

"I don't want to fight," I say again. "I'll let her up as long as we don't fight." Silence. More silence. Nothing to do but let her go. She's on me again and I pin her down again, and the gang surrounds us and I let her go again. This time I don't head out of the park.

The gang leader is saying, "If you leave now, we won't hurt you," but I can't. I shake my head and sit where two benches meet. Tears slide down my cheeks. The leader sits next to me and the others sit down beside him and beside me. I don't talk. I don't look at them.

He takes out a tissue and offers it to me. "Hey," he says, "what are you reading?" He takes my book, looks at the cover, and leafs through the pages. "Good?" he asks. I shrug my shoulders. We sit in silence and time goes by.

Suddenly, he snaps his fingers and everyone in the gang stands up. They linger until he gives a signal and together they walk off toward Avenue D. I sit a while longer, claiming my right to be there. Then I walk slowly out of the park, back to the apartment, and cry.

Parasites at Work

LOOKING THROUGH A PILE OF OLD MAGAZINES, I come across an issue of *Discover* with a picture of a hookworm magnified 500 times on its cover and a lead article entitled *Do Parasites Rule the World?*

The first organism described is the *Sacculina Carcini*, a parasite that does not inspire "immediate respect," but who, biologists now recognize, "is a powerhouse in disguise." The more I read, the more I'm thinking, "This sounds just like the Bush administration."

I consult Webster's Dictionary and find that a parasite is "a person who lives at the expense of others without making any useful contribution or return... [or] a plant or animal that lives on or within another organism from which it derives sustenance or protection without making compensation. Wow! The Bush administration fulfills both definitions, and it is, amazingly, the human equivalent of the *Sacculina Carcini* in its perpetuation of self at the cost of the integrity and well-being of its host.

The *Sacculina Carcini* begins as a larva swimming about in search of its host. Sensing one in the form of a crab, the female approaches, finds a weakness in the crab's exoskeleton, and injects herself into the crab's body. The Bush administration in its larval stage wanders about the country looking for a weakness in its host, the body politic of the United States. It finds one in the electoral system, which it manipulates in states such as Florida, and injects itself into power through it.

Once inside, the *Sacculina* sends tendrils throughout the host's body to draw in nutrients as it begins to grow. The administration, once inside, sends out tendrils through appointments of like-minded judges, self-serving legislation, and placement of its own people in influential positions. These tendrils bring nutrients to the parasitic administration in the forms of wealth, power, and control.

After the parasite is firmly implanted, the host crab no longer has a life of her own, with her own pursuits and reproductive capacity. She stops growing and reproducing as her life is hijacked and she keeps consuming to feed the parasite. The Bush administration likewise changes its host's behavior. The country's self-regulatory system, based on the Constitution and Bill of Rights, is altered so that it no longer functions according to its original nature. Instead of operating in accordance with the country's "genetic" code of laws and values, the parasite creates The Patriot Act, for example, which takes away basic freedoms inherent to the host's character and perpetuation of self.

Reaching the *Sacculina's* level of success, the parasitic administration securely harnesses its host's resources to serve its own interests. For example, the host is sent to war to support the parasite's oil-based economic aspirations instead of developing its own alternative energy resources. Its enormous economic resources are allocated to the parasite's wars of choice instead of to its own need for social services, education, housing, and health.

As with the host crab, the host country's job becomes one of endless consumption to feed the parasites. George W. Bush securely tied consumption to patriotism after 9/11 when he declared that the way to help the nation was to "buy, buy, buy."

Much of the country is no longer conscious that it is serving the parasitic administration, just as the crab is not conscious that it is serving the *Sacculina Carcini*. Through propaganda disseminated through a collaborative media, the parasites have convinced many members of its host that it is working for them and not for themselves. Many vote against their self-interest and give their lives to support the parasitic administration and the corporations with which it is entwined.

Will the minority who remember the introduction of the parasite through the weak spot, who are tracking its takeover, be able to produce a successful and systemic immune response, or will the United States, like the crab, become merely a shell of its former self and live only to serve the parasites in power?

Security

A businessman in a starched peach shirt,
an old woman in sneakers,
a college student in hiking boots

all tying their shoes
after passing through security,

a skill they learned
as little girls and boys
leaning against their mothers
before going out to play.

Thai Tofu

I'M THINKING, *AIRPORT FOOD IS SO EXPENSIVE, so sterile, soggy, and plastic. How great it would be to bring some tasty food with me.* So I make sure to go to Green Fields Market to pick up Thai tofu, cubes of firm tofu in a spicy peanut sauce, great with good bread and fresh water. The water, of course, will have to wait. No liquids of any kind over 3 ounces can be carried on board, the airline emphasized in a message on my answering machine.

I arrive at the airport where a man takes my luggage outside the terminal and I head for the security checkpoint. Off come the shoes and bracelet, the change from my pockets, my knapsack. No alarms as I pass through the detection box. Very easy.

"Whose knapsack is this?" asks a small uniformed woman.

"Mine," I say.

"Step this way, please. Stand behind that line and do not attempt to touch your knapsack in any way."

I stand behind a metal shield as she gingerly unzips my pack. Out come a book, a scarf, lozenges, the Thai tofu. She picks the container up between gloved fingers and holds it to the light. She squeezes it gently to get a sense of its consistency. She consults with another guard. The Homeland Security badge on her sleeve gets my attention.

"We have to keep this," she says. "The consistency is unacceptable."

"It's tofu," I tell her. "It's delicious."

"I'm sorry. You can go back into the terminal and eat it there, but it cannot go any further."

"That's okay. You should eat it though. It's really good."

"We cannot consume anything we retain," she replies.

I put my shoes on, gather my things, hesitate, and then walk on. I am sad to leave this tofu, an unlikely casualty in the war on terror.

Addressing Speciesism in the Classroom

"... the time is coming when people will be amazed that the human race existed so long before it recognized that thoughtless injury to life is incompatible with real ethics. Ethics is in its unqualified form extended responsibility to everything that has life." —Albert Schweitzer, humanitarian and Nobel Peace Prize recipient

S PECIESISM IS ONE OF THE LAST WIDELY-HELD preju-
dices to remain unquestioned and institutionalized
in society-at-large. It is a belief system in which
Homo Sapiens consider themselves superior to all other
species and feel justified in giving those species few, if any,
rights.

To some, combating speciesism is a fringe issue. To
others, it is essential to human morality and to the ability
of people to live in peace, not only with other animals but
also with each other. Native Americans teach that the
lives of humans and animals are inextricably intertwined,
we are all one, and what we do to other living beings, we
do to ourselves. Philosophies, such as Buddhism, teach
respect for all living beings.

Many great scientists, doctors, artists, and religious
and political leaders throughout the history of western
civilization have also advocated respect for animals and
rejected exploitation of them. Unfortunately, their
perceptions and attitudes are still absent from standard

textbooks and therefore from general consciousness. We can, however, reclaim this heritage and encourage respect for animals by incorporating their ideas throughout our curricula.

There are so many animal advocates in each discipline. Here are the words of some of them.

Alice Walker: "The animals of the world exist for their own reasons. They were not made for humans any more than black people were made for whites, or women created for men."

President Abraham Lincoln: "I am in favor of animal rights as well as human rights. That is the way of the whole human being."

Leonardo da Vinci: "The time will come when men such as I will look upon the murder of animals as now they look upon the murder of men."

Charles Darwin: "The love for all living creatures is the most noble attribute of man."

St. Francis of Assisi: "Not to hurt our humble brethren is our first duty to them, but to stop there is not enough. We have a higher mission — to be of service to them wherever they require it."

Values such as these, when introduced to students, can inspire respect for animals.

In addition, teachers can expose the prejudice toward animals in our language. People routinely refer to an animal as 'it', even though the individual is as female and male as any human being. By replacing 'it' with the appropriate pronoun 'he' or 'she,' animals can emerge in human consciousness as living beings with individual lives as parents, children, siblings, and members of social groups.

Teachers can also help students understand the reality behind euphemisms. Sport hunting, for example, is a euphemism for killing or murder. If a human shoots another person without the justification of self-defense or survival, it is called cold-blooded murder. When a person shoots an animal without similar justification, it is called sport hunting. The former is considered horrifying and demands punishment, the latter is considered routine and rarely has consequences. Because we human beings are in control of our language, we create words to give more value to our species and less value to others. These words reflect respect for human life and disregard for the lives of other animals. As these euphemisms arise in class, teachers can help students explore the reality they obfuscate.

Another linguistic feature that teachers can address is the use of negative similes, such as "acting just like an animal." When people do something particularly horrible, people say they are "acting like animals" when, in fact, they are acting like human beings. Other animals do not commit horrendous crimes like imprisonment, torture, rape, and widespread gratuitous killing. Therefore, the accurate phrase should be, he or she is acting "just like a human being."

Lastly, to address speciesism, teachers need to model non-speciesist behavior in the classroom. When students or teachers see an insect or spider, the usual reaction is to kill that being. The message teachers convey by either doing or allowing the killing is that if you are bigger, stronger, and can get away with it, killing is the way to solve conflicts of interest. However, I have watched student behavior change after abiding by the class rule that no living being can be harmed during class and after watching me catch and release a bee or spider or open a window to allow a fly to escape. By the end of the semester, the students are doing the catching and releasing and telling each other to do no harm.

Such modeling demonstrates that there are peaceful ways to solve problems, that might does not make right, that each life is of value, and that there are simple, everyday actions one can take to honor lives that seem different from our own. Although there are times when one must act in self-defense, those times are rare, while acts of unnecessary violence, such as the above, are routine.

As teachers we can demonstrate respect and empathy not only in our dealings with one another, but in our interactions with all other species as well. As Albert Einstein said, "Our task must be to free ourselves by widening our circle of compassion to embrace all living creatures and the whole of nature in its beauty."

Mantra of Those Who Have

My oil, my air, my water, my fish
My money, my stocks, my profits, my fists
My insurance, my family, my children, my plans
My house, my planet, my soft white hands.

My car, my food, my friends, my trees
My cocktails, my image, my meat, my seas
My wars, my brands, my stomach, my pride
My violence, my rights, my god on my side.

I've got it all,
you don't,
how sad.

I deserve it.
You don't.

Too bad.

Things to Carry

I ALWAYS CARRY SOMETHING: books for school, money, the chiropractor schedule, my credit card, my fear, my past – so many stories to lug around.

My friend carries half her house every time she goes out: bottles of water, art supplies, snacks, a camera, maps – she sags and staggers under the weight.

The birds at my feeder carry away enough sunflower seeds in a few hours to fill a small hollow tree. Back and forth, back and forth, so focused, they narrowly miss my head if I'm sitting in their flight path.

And then there are the Thai elephants who are forced to carry tourists up and down the beaches, the ones who knew the tsunami was coming, who broke their chains, kneeled to the ground, and voluntarily carried people to safety high into the hills.

And there are those coming back from Iraq carrying the memories of war, who will carry these memories their whole lives as they move through a society that refuses to carry the responsibility for having ruined so many lives.

Laura Plantation, New Orleans 2005

The plantation house is two stories high,
with splashes of bright color
and a sweeping verandah.

The slave quarters are around back,
wooden shacks with small porches
holding peeling, creaky chairs.
.
The fields have shrunk,
the last slaves liberated a hundred and forty years ago,
the last workers gone by 1977.

I walk across the worn
front porch of a slave cabin
through a sparse, small kitchen
into the back room.

It is dim and dusty, quiet,
hard to make out the shape
hanging from the ceiling.

I move closer.
It's a birdcage
with wooden slats and screening
ensuring no escape.

This morning I saw a slave auction block
in a New Orleans museum,
its wood worn
by the thousands of feet
that had walked and stood there,
by the knees of those
who had pleaded and cried there.

Now I hear the flutter of ghostly wings,
see the marks left by the tiny feet
forced to cling to a wooden bar
in this cage,
built by the enslaved.

Marx and Horney

KARL MARX AND KAREN HORNEY were both deeply concerned with the profound sense of alienation that arises from disturbed interpersonal relationships. For Marx, this alienation originates in the vast inequity between owners and workers in a capitalist system. For Horney, it is a result of the misuse of power within families. In both systems, those with less power experience the loss of personal control, resulting in feelings of isolation, anxiety, helplessness, low self-esteem, and an inaccurate sense of self-interest.

Although Marx found the source of alienation in the relationship between workers and owners, while Horney located it in the relationships between parents and children, the dynamics and effects within the dysfunctional systems of capitalism and neurotic families are amazingly similar.

In the conceptual points of convergence below, the alienated refer to both workers and neurotics, while the systems refer to capitalism and neurosis. The dominant forces are corporate owners, parents, and compulsive intra-psychic drives. From this brief review, one can see that indeed "the political is personal and the personal is political."

≈ the alienated are divorced from the decision-making process;

≈ the alienated experience a fundamental anxiety from feeling isolated and helpless in a hostile world;

≈ alienation results in low self-esteem;

≈ the alienated participate in the system compulsively and unconsciously;

≈ false consciousness and unconsciousness separate the alienated from their real feelings, perceptions, desires, self-interest, and full potential;

≈ the alienated do whatever is needed to keep the structure intact so they can feel safe;

≈ while the systems exhibit inconsistencies and surface conflicts which point to underlying conflicts, the alienated do not address the underlying causes, but keep producing pseudo-solutions that mask the real problems and the reasons for them;

≈ the dominant forces use scapegoating, externalization, rationalization, and idealization to promote their own interests;

≈ the dominant forces control ideological production in order to maintain the status quo;

≈ the sense of alienation permeates the entire system;

≈ the alienated are motivated to address their false consciousness or unconsciousness when the promise of the system fails to deliver even though they are doing "everything right";

≈ the alienated can be given tools – political education or therapy - to increase awareness of their situation and their true self-interest, and to help them organize into a power that can overcome repressive forces.

The Pile

Take the individual out of the pile, you said,
take the individual out of the pile.

You were referring to the heaps of Jews
thrown into human hills,
their stories as indistinguishable
as taut skin over dead bones.

The mountains of war dead,
of the starving and sick,
of the old and the different,
of the billions in slaughterhouses,
the list goes on and on.

So many souls
to be resurrected
from the dust of our indifference.

Requirements for Those Holding Public Office

Office Holders must:

- ≈ live by the laws of the land;
- ≈ be tried for murder, if allowing any policy that causes death to another;
- ≈ be tried for robbery, if allowing any policy that impoverishes;
- ≈ receive the minimum hourly wage;
- ≈ conduct business outside under trees wearing minimal, but sufficient, clothing;
- ≈ receive the minimal health benefits allowed by law;
- ≈ be the first to fight in any war they support;
- ≈ send their children to the worst schools;
- ≈ visit a slaughterhouse weekly;
- ≈ live next door to a nuclear power plant;
- ≈ eat only what they can buy using food stamps;
- ≈ be homeless for two months;
- ≈ drink the water from the most polluted water sources in the nation;
- ≈ write a haiku every morning;
- ≈ be in therapy;
- ≈ spend one month in a maximum security prison in solitary confinement;
- ≈ watch the sun rise and set in silence everyday;
- ≈ live in drug-infested neighborhoods;
- ≈ receive in retirement only social security benefits based on the lowest income bracket;
- ≈ take a ten day silent meditation retreat once a year;

≈ live in rat-infested apartments with no heat;
≈ abstain from alcohol and tobacco and smoke marijuana if they need a recreational drug;
≈ go on a vision quest in the wilderness;
≈ take truth serum and be questioned on domestic and foreign policy.

The Sanctity of Motherhood

I just read your poem,
about being nothing in your child body,
but something when you birthed your children,
nothing again as you age.

Perhaps you think of yourself
as a vessel empty – full – empty.
I don't know
so I have some questions.

Is a mother who sends her children to war
something,
and a peacemaking woman without children
nothing?

Is a mother who raises her children
to thoughtlessly consume
something,
and a woman without children
who honors all life
nothing?

Is a mother who neglects her children
something,
and a woman without children
working a lifetime helping children
nothing?

Tell me, what were you thinking?

They Took My Heart

I. THE RODENT

They took my heart
It hangs in that vial
Washed with soap
It beats no more

They took my heart
In this laboratory
That glass case
Is now its home

They took my heart
Look what they're doing
Giving some air
Like when I last breathed

They took my heart
They are giving it blood
Like what flowed through me
When I was alive

They took my heart
They're giving it cells
Like my body gave
All by itself

They took my heart
Now it beats again
In that glass vial
Alone without me

II. The Scientist

Well, we wanted to build a heart, but it's so complex, so
we decided to take a rodent's heart and wash it clean and
keep the scaffolding. See. The heart is actually gelatinous
when all its cells have been washed with just common
soap. Well, we introduced some oxygen and blood and it
started to look more alive and then we introduced the stem
cells. Now stem cells can become anything, so once we
introduced them into the heart tissue, they became heart
cells that expand and contract. It was the most amazing
moment of my life when my assistant called and said, "Are
you ready for this? The heart is beating again!"

III. The Rodent

They took my heart
Now it beats again
In that glass vial
Alone without me

Dodge Poetry Festival 2008
Waterloo, New Jersey

Here in this place where poets speak
the distillation of their souls,
held in words grasped in last night's darkness
or in books of years ago,
I stand in this graveyard behind a restored church
in this old remnant town of Waterloo.

51 years 2 months
2 years 10 months
84 years for husband and wife
lying side by side beneath this drizzling rain.

Citizens during the uncivil Civil War,
what did you say when you had breath and vibrating flesh
to bring yourselves into the world?

Did you declare your truth,
praise creation, denounce slavery?

Whatever your words, they have touched our lives,
as the sigh of a lover or a shout of fear
creates a breeze or a storm in places unseen,
as our words here today shape the lives yet to be.

In this, our time of war, time of greed,
the words of poets disperse from these tents,
seeking their sisters and brothers
imprisoned in lies, buried alive in graves of mass deception.

"Let us out!" the prisoners cry,
rattling the bars, pounding the lids
of their coffins, "Let us out!"

And the poems that fill this autumn air answer,
        we are searching for you,
                we will find you,
                        we will set you free.

Acknowledgements

A special thank you to

Morgan Kelner and Bernice Mennis for their
editorial and financial assistance,
Liz Kelner for her consistent and enthusiastic support,
Pilar for her friendship and love,
and Maureen Moore of Booksmyth Press
who brought this book into being.

ABOUT THE TYPE

The text of this book
was set in Perpetua OTF, the digital version of a
classic, sensitive text face widely used in quality
books. It was created in 1928 by the
famed British type designer
Eric Gill.

Made in the USA
Charleston, SC
01 November 2012